Milly, Mo
and
Salt and Pepper

"We may look different
but we feel the same."

Salt and Pepper are two old horses.

"Why did you name them Salt and Pepper?" Milly and Molly asked Farmer Hegarty one day. "Because of their colours," he said, "and because they are always together."

"Can we please ride them?" Milly and Molly asked.

"Of course you can," said Farmer Hegarty. "Salt and Pepper are the most trustworthy old horses I know."

"Salt and Pepper will clip-clop out but they will always clippity-clop home," warned Farmer Hegarty. "It's the clippity that will bounce you off. You must remember to hang on tightly coming home."

Milly and Molly went clip-clop, clip-clop, clip-clop down the road until they met Jack and Harry.

"Can we please come too?" they asked.

Salt and Pepper didn't mind.
Clip-clop, clip-clop, clip-clop.

And then they met Meg and Sophie.
"Can we please come too?" they asked.

Salt and Pepper didn't mind.
Clip-clop, clip-clop, clip-clop.

And then they met Tom and George.
"Can we please come too?" they asked.

Salt and Pepper didn't mind.
Clip-clop, clip-clop, clip-clop.

The day was an amble...

and a rosy red apple...

until it was time to go home.

Clippity-clop, clippity-clop, clippity-clop.
Tom and George bounced off at their gate.

Clippity-clop, clippity-clop, clippity-clop.
Meg and Sophie bounced off at their gate.

Clippity-clop, clippity-clop, clippity-clop.
Jack and Harry bounced off at their gate.

Clippity-clop, clippity-clop, clippity-clop.
But Milly and Molly didn't bounce off.
They hung on tightly until all of a sudden...

...Humphrey came around the corner on his bicycle, ringing his bell.

Milly and Molly closed their eyes.
Farmer Hegarty threw his hands up in horror.
But Salt and Pepper didn't mind.

They slowed down to a clippity-clop, clip-clop and stopped.

"Salt and Pepper," said Farmer Hegarty, "you are the most trustworthy old horses I know."